7 SECRETS
of the
EUCHARIST

7 Secrets
of the
Eucharist

Vinny Flynn

Introduction by Fr. Mitch Pacwa, S.J.

MercySong

STOCKBRIDGE, MASSACHUSETTS

PUBLISHED BY MERCYSONG, INC.
Stockbridge, Massachusetts USA
www.mercysong.com

IN COLLABORATION WITH IGNATIUS PRESS
Exclusive Distributor
San Francisco, California, USA

Library of Congress Control No: 2006937788

ISBN-10: 1-884479-31-6
ISBN-13: 978-1-884479-31-1

Cover design by Riz Boncan Marsella
PRINTED IN THE UNITED STATES OF AMERICA

December 2006

To Fr. George
"Praised be the Lord Jesus Christ!"

$\mathcal{C}$ONTENTS

INTRODUCTION

In reflecting on the Eucharist as the "source and summit" of our faith after the Second Vatican Council, Catholics sought hard to make the Eucharist relevant to the modern world. But, all too often, a fear that the Eucharist did not relate to modern experience led to an overemphasis on the community aspects of liturgy and a de-emphasis on individual worship.

Then in the 1980's, we witnessed the beginnings of a revival of Eucharistic adoration on a popular level. There was a renewed interest in greater accuracy in the translations of the Eucharistic texts and deeper theological reflection on the Eucharist as the re-presentation of Christ's sacrifice on Calvary. Young people were drawn in greater numbers to find meaning in Christ's real presence on the altar. They came to find Jesus in the Eucharist.

Part of the genius of this book is its ability to summon all Catholics to this deeper relationship with

Jesus Christ hidden in the Eucharist. Many Catholics are like the people of Nazareth at the time of Jesus. The divinity hiding in a hard-working carpenter who cared for his widowed Mother went mostly unnoticed in town — unnoticed until he announced himself in the synagogue as the fulfillment of Isaiah's prophecy (See Is 61: 1-2).

Though amazed at his words, the townsfolk lacked an expectant faith in what Christ could do or be, so when he rebuked them for their lack of faith, they rose up in fury to throw him over a cliff. But the hidden presence of his Person overcame their decision. He "passed through the midst of them" (Lk 4:30) and went on to amaze other towns with his wisdom and power.

This book is helpful because it takes the reader through the author's own personal questions about Christ's hidden presence. We are drawn into his growing awareness and insight into the amazing secrets of the Eucharist. His step-by-step deepening of faith helps the reader to follow the same path in discovering Christ's hidden presence.

One of the keys to bringing the soul into a faith-filled union with the Eucharistic Lord Jesus is the virtue of humility. The Nazarenes thought they had Jesus figured out. They had categories to keep him in his place since they knew his family, their simple occupation and social status. While the limitations of their "knowledge" kept the full truth of Jesus hidden, the author of this book uses the Church's fount of knowledge — continually citing the *Catechism of the Catholic Church*, the Councils, Popes and saints, particularly St. Faustina — in order to help us, his readers, acquire deeper wisdom and appropriate it as our own.

Another tremendous service of *7 Secrets of the Eucharist* is the way St. Faustina's Diary is integrated into the theme of the Eucharist. Vinny Flynn has been instrumental in introducing millions of people to the Divine Mercy message, through his writings and talks, and through the video of his family praying the Chaplet.

This book highlights the Eucharistic aspects of St. Faustina's simply expressed, yet tremendously profound teachings in order to engage the reader in the intimately personal union with Jesus Christ that the Saint revealed in her Diary. Vinny's reflections from the Diary do not take the reader back to the first third of the twentieth century, but apply the Saint's insights to contemporary concerns for meeting the Lord Jesus who is veiled in the Eucharist.

Perhaps influenced by St. Faustina's approach to the spiritual life, the author presents very profound insights into the Holy Eucharist in clear, simple ways.

We all need books like this one to help us grow spiritually, to remind us of what we are doing in the Mass, and to summon us to receive Jesus Christ in the Eucharist with fuller awareness and participation in the infinite mystery that remains always beyond the total grasp of our minds and hearts.

Fr. Mitch Pacwa, S.J.

INTRODUCTION

Author's Note

Quotations used in the text are generally arranged by page number and section in the Notes at the end. Quotations from Scripture, *The Catechism of the Catholic Church*, certain Church documents, and the Diary of St. Faustina are cited in the text itself.

Why St. Faustina?

Canonized by Pope John Paul II, April 30, 2000, Faustina became the first saint of the Jubilee Year that ushered in the third millennium. In his homily, the pope repeatedly referred to her as "a gift of God for our time." Known as the "Apostle of Divine Mercy," she is also one of the greatest saints of the Eucharist. Her religious name is Maria Faustina Kowalska of the Most Blessed Sacrament, and almost every page of her Diary contains some reference to the Eucharist.

Faustina called the Eucharist the "secret of my sanctity." May this book help you to discover why and to let the Eucharist lead you to sanctity as well.

FOREWORD

Beyond the Veil

> **O Jesus, hidden God,**
> **my heart perceives You**
> **though veils hide You.**
>
> *St. Faustina, Diary, 524*

All my life, the mystery that has drawn me most is the mystery of the Eucharist, the mystery of God with us, hidden by veils of bread and wine.

I know I will never understand it, and that's okay. But my whole life has been a continual exploration of this mystery, a kind of spiritual treasure hunt beyond the veil. This book is an attempt to share some of the treasures I've found along the way and invite you to continue the journey.

7 Secrets?

Don't be misled by the number 7 in the title. I don't mean to imply that there are only 7 or that there is any magic number of truths about the Eucharist. I've simply selected the ones that seem most basic and necessary as starting points of discovery. This is just a beginning, a first exploration beyond the veil.

The word "secrets" needs some clarification, too. There's nothing really new here, no real secrets. The truths I want to share with you have always been at the heart of the Church, embraced as precious gems by theologians, saints, and mystics.

I call them secrets because, for some reason, they don't seem to have been passed on to the average lay person in a way that would enable us to really understand them and incorporate them into our daily lives.

The Emmaus Problem

Our lack of understanding is nothing new. Even Christ's closest friends didn't understand. Remember the Emmaus story? Two of the disciples are walking from Jerusalem to the nearby village of Emmaus, confused and depressed, discussing the tragic events of the preceding days.

They had been hoping that Christ was the promised redeemer of Israel, but then, suddenly, He had been betrayed, arrested, tortured, and crucified.

Now, to add to the confusion, some of the women had come to them with an amazing story that the tomb was empty and that they had seen angels who told them Christ was alive.

Even though Christ had, on at least three occasions, predicted His passion, death, and resurrection, somehow it hadn't clicked with them. And so, as they walk along the road, they rehash it all, trying to make some sense out of it in the face of all their dashed hopes and unanswered questions.

Christ joins them on the road, but they don't

recognize Him. When they tell Him about the events they've been discussing, He chides them for their foolishness and failure to believe. He then explains the scriptures to them so powerfully that their hearts are burning within them, but they still don't realize who He is.

Finally, at "the breaking of the bread," their eyes are opened, and they recognize Him (Lk 24:13-35).

Come and see

I'm convinced that, like the disciples, most of us suffer, to some extent, from the Emmaus problem. Even though all the necessary details have been given to us in the teachings of the Church, we just haven't been able to put it all together. We don't fully recognize who this is whom we receive in the Eucharist, why He has given us this unique sacrament, or what kind of response He expects from us.

At each Mass, the priest says, "Behold the Lamb of God," an echo of what John the Baptist said to two of his disciples as Jesus walked by. When the disciples then began to follow Jesus, they asked Him,

"Where do you live?" and He replied, "Come and see" (Jn 1:39 *NJB*).

That's the invitation I'd like to pass along through this book, a simple invitation to take a closer look at the Eucharist, to come and see where the Master lives beyond the veil.

$\mathscr{S}$ECRET 1

The Eucharist is alive.

When I come to a human heart in Holy Communion, my hands are full of all kinds of graces which I want to give to the soul, but souls do not even pay attention to me. They leave me to myself and busy themselves with other things. ... They treat me as a dead object.

St. Faustina, Diary, 1385

The Eucharist is *alive*. That may seem obvious to you. I guess it was to me, at some intellectual level, but somehow I never really thought very deeply about what that actually meant.

The Eucharist is *alive*. If a stranger who knew nothing about the Eucharist were to watch the way we receive, would he know this? When you and I approach the Eucharist, does it look like we believe we are about to take into our bodies the *living person*, Jesus Christ, true God and true man?

How many times, Lord, have I forgotten that the Eucharist is alive! As I wait in line to receive you each day, am I thinking about how much you want to unite yourself with me? Am I seeing your hands filled with graces you want to give me? Am I filled with awe and gratitude that you love me so much as to actually want to come to me in this incredibly intimate way?

Or am I distracted, busy with other thoughts, preoccupied with myself and my agendas for the day? How many times, Jesus, have I made you sad, mindlessly receiving you into my body, into my heart, with no love and no recognition of your love? How many times have I treated you as a *dead object?*

The Host that we receive is not a thing! It's not a wafer! It's not bread! It's a *person* — and He's *alive!*

I'm afraid that, in many of our churches, a

stranger in our midst, witnessing a typical Sunday liturgy, would not realize this, but would simply see a bunch of people get up from their seats, wait in line, receive a piece of bread, and then go back to their seats.

All too often, as Christ says to St. Faustina, that's all it is for us. We go up and get something and then go back to our seats — back to our daily routines — without any real change taking place, without any deeper union with Christ, without any new awareness of His life within us.

In contrast to this, there's another scene, one that helps me remember how we *ought* to approach the Eucharist.

In 1916, as a year of preparation for Our Lady's appearances at Fatima, the Angel of Peace appeared three times to Lucia, Jacinta, and Francisco.

The most dramatic scene is the third visit, when the angel comes with the Eucharist. Suspending the Host and the chalice in the air, he throws himself prostrate on the ground and has the children repeat the following prayer three times:

Most Holy Trinity, Father, Son, and Holy Spirit, I offer You the most precious Body, Blood, Soul, and Divinity of Jesus Christ, present in all the tabernacles of the world, in reparation for the outrages, sacrileges, and indifference with which He Himself is offended. And, through the infinite merits of His most Sacred Heart and the Immaculate Heart of Mary, I beg of You the conversion of poor sinners.

An *angel* prostrates himself on the ground! *We* stand in line with our minds filled with distractions, walk up and receive Communion, return to our pews, and go back to "business as usual," thinking about the football game, or the bills we have to pay, or what we're going to do after Mass.

But an angel, a pure spirit, who lives constantly in the intimate presence of God, *prostrates* himself before the Eucharist in adoration!

That's a pretty strong message. It was so strong that young Francisco spent the rest of his short life trying to console God in the Eucharist. Every moment he could, he spent in front of the Blessed

Sacrament, trying to console God for the indifferent way that people respond to the Eucharist.

So there's our invitation; there's the contrast for us. We can treat God as a dead object, or we can prostrate our whole beings in front of Him, in adoration, in gratitude, in love, in reparation.

I'm not suggesting that we all run up and throw ourselves on our faces in front of the Eucharist the next time we go to receive. But *interiorly* we can. Whether we stand or kneel to receive, we can always, in our hearts, minds, and souls, be prostrate in adoration of the living God in the Eucharist.

As the Sacred Congregation for the Sacraments and Divine Worship explains:

> The Church has always required from the faithful respect and reverence for the Eucharist at the moment of receiving it.
>
> *Inaestimabile Donum,* 11

More and more people, feeling a need to express this reverence for Jesus in a concrete way as they go to receive, while also trying to avoid calling attention to themselves or disrupt the order of Communion, make a slight bow just before they receive.

For me, this has become a way to acknowledge Jesus in a personal way, with my whole being, not just my mind. And it fulfills the specific instructions given by the Church:

> When the faithful communicate kneeling, no other sign of reverence towards the Blessed Sacrament is required, since kneeling is itself a sign of adoration. When they receive Communion standing, it is strongly recommended that, coming up in procession, they should make a sign of reverence before receiving the Sacrament.
>
> *Inaestimabile Donum,* 11

As Pope John Paul II points out, we "need to cultivate a lively awareness of Christ's real presence," and we should take care "to show that awareness through tone of voice, gestures, posture, and bearing."

Pope Benedict XVI also discusses this issue of how to receive, emphasizing that, instead of arguing about whether it's better to receive kneeling or standing, in the hand or on the tongue, we need to focus on the spirit of reverence with which the early

Fathers of the Church received Communion.

First urging priests to "exercise tolerance and to recognize the decision of each person," he goes on to ask everyone "to exercise the same tolerance and not to cast aspersions on anyone who may have opted for this or that way of doing it." What is important is reverence:

> It is quite wrong to argue about this or that form of behavior. We should be concerned only to argue in favor of ... a reverence in the heart, an inner submission before the mystery of God.

I think part of the reason why this reverence is so often missing and Christ is so often treated as a dead object is that the words we use can sometimes get in our way. How many times have we heard the priest repeat over and over as he distributes Communion, "the Body of Christ ... the Body of Christ ... the Body of Christ ..."?

In our culture, the word *body* doesn't usually suggest fullness of life. What it always brought to my mind was the *dead* body of Christ, the body hanging on the cross. And, after all, doesn't the Church teach that the Mass is the sacrifice of Calvary re-presented, rendered present in our time and place?

Yes. But the cross is meaningless without the resurrection.

This is *not* the dead Christ locked in a moment of time on the cross. This is the *complete* and eternal Christ, the Christ who was born of the Virgin, who came into our midst, suffered, died, was *raised* from the dead, and *is now fully alive* in heaven, where He reigns in glory.

"The flesh of the Son of Man, given as food," explains Pope John Paul II, "is his body in its glorious state after the resurrection."

The *"Credo" of the People of God* states this very clearly:

> We believe that as the bread and wine consecrated by the Lord at the Last Supper were changed into His body and His blood, which were to be offered for us on the cross, likewise the bread and wine consecrated by the priest are changed into the body and blood of Christ, *enthroned gloriously in heaven.*

And the *Catechism of the Catholic Church* adds:

> Under the consecrated species of bread and wine, Christ himself, *living and glorious*, is present in a true, real, and substantial manner.
>
> #1413

It is this living and glorious Christ who complains to St. Faustina:

> **Oh, how painful it is to me that souls so seldom unite themselves to me in Holy Communion. I wait for souls and they are indifferent toward me. I love them tenderly and sincerely and they distrust me. I want to lavish my graces on them and they do not want to accept them. They treat me as a dead object, whereas my heart is full of love and mercy.**
>
> *Diary*, 1447

The Eucharist is not a thing. It is not a dead object. It is Christ, and He is *fully alive*. Receiving Him with this awareness, we become more fully alive, so that we can say with St. Paul, "It is no longer I who live, but Christ who lives in me" (Gal 2:20 *RSV*).

> I am the *living* bread. ... Whoever eats
> this bread will *live* forever. ... Just as the
> *living* Father sent me and I have *life* because
> of the Father, so also the one who feeds on
> me will have *life* because of me.
>
> Jn 6: 51, 57

> My heart is drawn there where my God
> is hiding. It is my *living* God though a veil
> hides Him.
>
> *Diary*, 1591

THE EUCHARIST IS ALIVE

SECRET 2

Christ is not alone.

*Jesus ... You come to me in Holy Communion,
You who together with the Father and the
Holy Spirit have deigned to dwell in the
little heaven of my heart. ...*

St. Faustina, Diary, 486

When He becomes present for us in the Eucharist, Christ is not alone. I don't know what you learned, but I never really learned this. Through years of CCD classes, Catholic high school, Catholic college, and homilies at daily Mass, no one ever even suggested to me that Christ does not become present alone.

I was so proud of myself. I thought I understood all there was to know about the Eucharist. I not only understood Transubstantiation; I could even spell it. I had learned that this strange word literally means *a crossing from one substance to another*, and that, as applied to the Eucharist, it refers to the most unique and complete crossing imaginable — that from the moment of consecration, the entire substance of the bread and wine ceases to exist, and that what still appears to our senses as bread and wine is now the body and blood of Christ:

> By the consecration of the bread and wine there takes place a change of the whole substance of the bread into the substance of the body of Christ our Lord and of the whole substance of the wine into the substance of His blood.
>
> Council of Trent, *CCC*, #1376

I could quote the teaching, but I didn't really understand it, didn't realize how much more there was to it, and had no clue that Christ is not alone.

Only when I started studying the Council of Trent's definition of the Eucharist did the veil start to lift. The Council teaches that the Eucharist contains "the body and blood, together with the soul and divinity, of our Lord Jesus Christ."

Together with the soul and divinity! Christ is present in the Eucharist with His body and blood together with His soul and divinity. What does that mean?

A deeper look at another mystery, the mystery of the Incarnation, provided the answer. Like many Catholics, I was familiar with the term Incarnation, but all I knew about it was that it referred to the moment in time when the second person of the Trinity "became incarnate," meaning, "took on human flesh" — the Son of God became man.

The Church teaches that at the words of Mary's *Fiat:* "Let it be done to me according to your word," a human nature, with a body and a soul, was created from her through the power of the Holy Spirit and was fused forever to the divine nature of the second person of the Trinity.

As the *Catechism* explains,

> [This] does not mean that Jesus Christ is part God and part man, nor does it imply that he is the result of a confused mixture of the divine and the human. He became truly man while remaining truly God.
>
> #464

Jesus Christ is *one* divine person with *two* distinct natures — one totally human, one totally divine. These two natures are so inseparable that the divine person of Christ "remained united to his soul and body, even when these were separated from each other by death" (*CCC* #650); and, when the Father raised Christ up, He "perfectly introduced His son's humanity, including His body, into the Trinity" (*CCC* #648).

How does this help us understand Christ's presence in the Eucharist?

As we saw in the previous chapter, our words can fool us. When we speak of the bread becoming the body of Christ and the wine becoming the blood of Christ, our words can imply — incorrectly — that this is all that happens and that Christ can be divided into parts.

By virtue of the words of consecration, the body of Christ does indeed become present under the appearances of bread, and the blood of Christ does indeed become present under the appearances of wine.

But we cannot divide Christ. Wherever His body is, His blood must also be. And wherever His body and blood are, His human soul and His divine nature must also be.

To explain this complete unity of Christ as one person with two inseparable natures, theologians use the term *concomitance*. By the words, "This is my body," the body of Christ becomes present. By concomitance, His blood, human soul, and divine nature become present *with* His body.

Likewise, by the words, "This is my blood," the blood of Jesus becomes present, and by concomitance His body, human soul, and divine nature become present *with* His blood.

Thus, the Church teaches that every particle of what looks like bread contains the entire Christ, and every drop of what looks like wine contains the entire Christ:

> Christ is present whole and entire in each of the species and whole and entire in each of their parts, in such a way that the breaking of the bread does not divide Christ.
>
> *CCC,* #1377

This is why we don't have to receive Communion under both species; in other words, under the forms of both the bread and the wine. If we receive under either form, we receive the whole Christ.

The whole Christ — in His complete humanity and His complete divinity. I was beginning to understand the humanity part of it, that His human body, blood, and soul are present together in the Eucharist. But what did it really mean that He is also present in His complete divinity?

With a new focus, I reread Pope Paul VI's encyclical letter on the Eucharist, *Mysterium Fidei,* and his great profession of faith, *The "Credo" of the People of God.* Two phrases jumped out at me: Christ is present in the Eucharist "as He is in heaven," and "without leaving heaven."

How is Christ present in heaven? Is He alone? Of course not!

Christ is the second person of the Blessed Trinity, true God and true man, eternally united with the Father and the Holy Spirit. Just as there can be no separation within Christ's human nature, so there can be none within His divine nature. Just as we cannot separate Christ's body from His blood, or His soul from His body and blood, so we cannot separate Christ from the other persons in the Trinity.

Time after time, we hear the priest pray to the Father at the end of the opening prayer of the Mass:

> We ask this through our Lord Jesus Christ, your Son, who lives and reigns with you and the Holy Spirit, one God, forever and ever.

In heaven, Christ "lives and reigns" together with the Father and the Holy Spirit.

And how does He reign?

As the Son of God and the Son of Man, the King

of Kings. Glorified now in body and soul and seated at the right hand of the Father, He is surrounded by the whole heavenly court of angels and saints, and eternally reunited with His Mother, the Blessed Virgin Mary who, having been assumed into heaven, body and soul, now reigns with Him as Queen of heaven and earth.

Christ is never alone. When He becomes present in the Eucharist as He is in heaven, without leaving heaven, that means that all of heaven is present with Him. No wonder He told us, "The kingdom of heaven is within you" (Lk 17: 21 *RSV*).

When I think now of what I used to believe, I have to laugh; it brings to mind such an absurd scene:

> Just another day in the Kingdom of Heaven. Christ looks quickly at His watch, jumps up from His throne, and grabs His best white robe: "Bye Dad, bye Mom, bye Holy Spirit, bye all you angels and saints. Gotta hurry down to earth now to be present in the Eucharist. I know you'll miss me, but I'll be back as soon as I can."

Christ doesn't leave heaven to be present in the

Eucharist, and His presence in the Eucharist is not different from His presence in heaven. There are many consecrated Hosts throughout the world, but Christ doesn't multiply Himself to be present in all those different places.

There is only one Christ, only one presence of Christ, only one way Christ exists:

> The unique and indivisible existence of the Lord glorious in heaven is not multiplied, but is rendered present by the Sacrament in the many places on earth where Mass is celebrated.
>
> *The "Credo" of the People of God*

What does all this mean for you and me?

It means that whenever we receive Communion, we enter into communion with the Holy Trinity.

Did anybody ever tell you that?

With each reception of Holy Communion, we experience, already here on earth, the same divine activity that we will one day experience in all its fullness in heaven — the divine activity of love eternally taking place within the Trinity.

As Father M.V. Bernadot, O.P. explains,

> The Word comes to us. But He does not come alone.
>
> "I am in the Father and the Father in me" (Jn 14:10). ... "He who sent me is with me. He has not left me alone" (Jn 8:29 *RSV*). ...
>
> Where the Father and the Son are present, the Holy Spirit is also there. Thus, the Blessed Trinity dwells in the heart of each person receiving Communion.
>
> Jesus Himself assures us of this:
>
> "If a man loves me, ... my Father will love him, and we will come to him and make our dwelling with him" (Jn 14:23 *RSV*).

"And make our dwelling with him." God wants to live His triune life in us. We are called to be dwelling places for the Holy Trinity and to enter into a personal relationship with each of the persons in God.

It's easy to get bogged down in the theological explanations of all this (which is perhaps why we don't hear a lot about it from the pulpit), because we're dealing with depths of mystery that our human understanding can never fully fathom. But there is an important theological distinction that needs to be made about the Eucharist and the Trinity.

Only Christ, the second person of the Trinity, was made flesh. Only Christ assumed a human nature. So, in this wonderful encounter with the Trinity, only Christ is present *sacramentally;* that is, under the appearances of bread and wine.

The Father and the Holy Spirit are not present *sacramentally,* but each is *really and truly present* with Christ because of the perfect unity of the Trinity.

What do we mean by *really and truly?*

Theologians use special terms to articulate and clarify the dogma of the Trinity, though the *Catechism* makes it clear that there can be no full explanation, because even these terms "... signify an ineffable mystery, infinitely beyond all that we can humanly understand" (251).

Using the principle of *consubstantiality,* the Church teaches that each person of the Trinity is consubstantial with the others, meaning that the Father and the Son and the Holy Spirit are *of the same divine nature or substance.* As the *Catechism* explains:

> The Trinity is One. We do not confess three Gods, but one God in three persons, the "consubstantial Trinity." The divine persons do not share one divinity among themselves but each of them is God whole and entire.
>
> #253

To this teaching, the Church adds the principle of *circumincession:* the mutual presence of the three Divine persons in one another — each is present in each other without ceasing to be distinct.

> The divine Unity is Triune. ... Because of that unity the Father is wholly in the Son and wholly in the Holy Spirit; the Son is wholly in the Father and wholly in the Holy Spirit; the Holy Spirit is wholly in the Father and wholly in the Son.
>
> *CCC, # 254, 255*

How does this all tie together?

In our earlier discussion of *concomitance,* we saw that Christ's divinity becomes present with His body and blood at the words of consecration. We have now learned that both the Father and the Holy Spirit are consubstantial with Christ (of the same divine nature); and that, by circumincession, each of the three persons is eternally present in each other while remaining distinct.

Thus, whenever we receive Christ sacramentally, under the form of bread or wine or both, the Father and the Holy Spirit become present *with* Him, not sacramentally but in a nonetheless true, complete, and substantial way.

Imagine a symbolic painting of the Trinity in heaven. The Father is seated on a throne with Jesus on a throne to His right. The dove, symbolic of the Holy Spirit, hovers above. Our Lady, as queen of heaven and earth, has an honored place near them, with all the saints and angels gathered round.

(Obviously, the picture is not accurate, because there is no way we can portray the great mystery that even though each person of the Trinity is distinct from the others, there is no separation between them; and that even though each saint is still an individual being, all are now one with each other and incorporated into the Trinity. See *CCC* #1023-1027).

Now imagine that, instead of seeing Jesus on the throne, you see a Host. The Father is still there, along with the Holy Spirit and all of heaven. Nothing has changed except that Jesus is hidden by a veil that looks like a wafer of bread.

When Jesus, "gloriously enthroned in heaven," is made present for us behind that veil, we can look beyond the veil and see not only Jesus, but the whole heavenly reality that surrounds Him.

When we consume the Communion wafer, which we call the "Host," Christ *is* the Host; the Father and the Holy Spirit are *with* the Host and live in us with Christ, joining us to themselves and all of heaven. "God the Trinity comes to meet us, becomes a God who is with us and among us."

How beautifully the *Catechism of the Catholic Church* expresses this reality:

> The whole Christian life is a communion with each of the divine persons, without in any way separating them. ... We are called to be a dwelling for the Most Holy Trinity.
>
> #259, 260

Many of the saints experienced this divine union, this indwelling of the Holy Trinity, in a very real and personal way. St. Faustina writes:

> Once after Holy Communion, I heard these words: **You are our dwelling place.** At that moment, I felt in my soul the presence of the Holy Trinity: the Father, the Son, and the Holy Spirit.
>
> *Diary,* 451

And again, during Eucharistic adoration:

> I knew more distinctly than ever before the Three Divine Persons, the Father, the Son, and the Holy Spirit. My soul is in communion with these Three. ... Whoever is united to One of the Three Persons is thereby united to the whole Blessed Trinity, for this Oneness is indivisible.
>
> *Diary,* 472

How grateful we should be for this wonderful gift of the Eucharist, through which God imparts the very life of the Trinity to us! With what awe and joy should we sing with St. Catherine of Siena:

Would it not have been enough to create us after Your own image and likeness, making us re-born through grace by the blood of Your Son? Was it still necessary that You should give even the Holy Trinity as food for our souls?

To St. Padre Pio, the Mass was not only Calvary but also Paradise, and the Blessed Virgin Mary was his constant companion at the altar. When asked about this, he explained that Our Lady is present at every Mass, along with all the angels and "the whole celestial court." At each Mass,

he saw the heavens open, the splendor of God, and the glory of the angels and saints.

St. Therese experienced this in a very personal way at the moment of her first Communion. As she prepared to receive Christ under the sacred species, the young mystic realized that, not only was the Trinity about to dwell in her but, since the saints and angels in heaven are "perfectly incorporated into

Christ" (*CCC*, #1026), all of heaven would come to her, too.

During the ceremony, she was moved to tears, which some people misinterpreted, thinking she was sad because her mother had died and wasn't there to share this special moment with her. Therese writes:

> It was beyond them that all the joy of heaven had entered one small, exiled heart, and that it was too weak to bear it without tears. As if the absence of my mother could make me unhappy on the day of my first Communion! As all of heaven entered my soul when I received Jesus, my mother came to me as well.

$\mathcal{S}$ECRET 3

There is only one Mass.

Oh, what awesome mysteries take place during Mass! ... One day we will know what God is doing for us in each Mass, and what sort of gift He is preparing in it for us. Only His divine love could permit that such a gift be provided for us.

St. Faustina, Diary, 914

Odds are that, right now, somewhere in the world, there's a priest celebrating Mass. As a matter of fact, there may be hundreds of Masses going on right now.

And they may be very different in a lot of ways.

There are so many possible differences, in fact, that most Catholics have developed a set of "Mass preferences." We each tend to prefer certain types of Masses over others, to the point that we may even "shop around" to find the Mass that suits us best.

Basically, we want to know things like, "Who's saying the Mass?" ... "Who's giving the homily?" ... "Who's doing the music?" ... "How do they distribute Communion?" ... "Do they have altar boys or altar girls?" ... "Do they stand or kneel?" ... Or even (I shudder to say it), "How long will it take?"

Some of us, especially those who are able to go to daily Mass, regular prayer meeting Masses, or special Masses in our homes, even get possessive about it, viewing each Mass as our own particular little Mass.

I think this must be a kind of "occupational hazard" for priests. You get used to your own church, your own people, your own style and customs, and it's easy to start to take ownership and get pulled into a microcosmic view of the liturgy.

Some priests even presume the right to adapt the text of the liturgy itself, making various wording changes that they feel will make the Mass more meaningful. The Mass becomes a forum for their own individual charisms, ideas, feelings, and beliefs, and a way to emphasize the things they feel are most important.

I'm reminded of a guest priest who came to say Mass at a prayer meeting a few years ago. He introduced the Mass by saying, "I don't know what you're used to doing here, but this is *my* Mass so we are going to do it this way. ..." And he listed certain things he wanted done in specific ways.

I remember thinking, "*My* Mass"? Can anyone really say, "*My* Mass"?

We tend to get so wrapped up in our own little worlds of time and space — and sometimes in our own philosophies, theologies, and preferences — that we fail to recognize the eternal, universal dimension of what's happening in the Mass. Just as there's a veil over the Eucharist, so too, there's a veil over the Mass itself, keeping us from seeing the awesome mystery we are being invited to enter.

So, before we go any further, we need to spend a little time talking about time — and about the

Eternal Now.

As human beings, we are subject to the limitations of time and space (along with matter and gravity). We tend to perceive events, not all at once, but sequentially, and our minds categorize each of them in terms of a particular place and time: past, present, or future.

Why the science lesson?

Because you probably won't understand the rest of this chapter without it.

Because of our limitations of time and space, you and I tend to view the crucifixion of Christ as simply an historic event, a tragic incident that happened at a particular time (roughly 2000 years ago) and in a particular place (Jerusalem).

It happened. Long ago and, for most of us, far away. We're sorry it happened. We may think about it a lot. We may use pictures and crosses to help us remember it. Hopefully, we try to learn from it and realize how much God loved us. But it's a past event. It happened once, and now it's over.

The problem is that God doesn't see it that way — and neither does the Church.

There is no time with God:

> With the Lord, one day is like a thousand years, and a thousand years are like one day.
>
> 2 Pet 3:8

The Church has always taught that God is unlimited, so He transcends time and space (along with matter and gravity). God sees everything — past, present, and future — all at once. For God, everything is always present; God lives in the Eternal Now.

How does this relate to the crucifixion?

Let's look at Church teaching. *The Catechism of the Catholic Church* makes it clear that Christ's passion, death, resurrection, and ascension should not be viewed merely as separate events, but rather as one unique event, which the Church calls "the Paschal mystery." And this Paschal mystery is not an event that can be assigned only to a particular time and place. It is not simply an event that took place 2000 years ago in Jerusalem and is now over.

> [The Paschal mystery is] the unique

event of history which does not pass away: Jesus dies, is buried, rises from the dead, and is seated at the right hand of the Father "once for all."

#1085

The *Catechism* goes on to explain that, though the Paschal mystery is an actual event that did occur in our history, it differs from all other historical events because they all happen once and then "pass away, swallowed up in the past" (#1085).

By contrast, the Paschal mystery "cannot remain only in the past:"

All that Christ is — all that He did and suffered for men — participates in the divine eternity, and so transcends all times while being present in them all. The event of the Cross and Resurrection abides and draws everything toward life.

#1085

What does this mean? It means that the sacrifice of the Eucharist, which we call the Mass, is never an isolated, individual event. Each time a Mass is offered it "makes present the one sacrifice of Christ" (#1330).

This is part of the miracle of the Mass, that it "not only recalls the events that saved us but actualizes them, makes them present. The Paschal mystery of Christ is celebrated, not repeated" (#1104), as the Church "re-lives the great events of salvation history in the 'today' of her liturgy" (#1095).

The priestly minister, then, presiding over the Eucharistic sacrifice, is not accomplishing anything new; but rather, through his ministry, the once-for-all sacrifice of the Cross, which is always present before the Father in heaven, *is now made present in our time and place.*

Thus, "the sacrifice of Christ and the sacrifice of the Eucharist are one single sacrifice" (#1367), and, as the Council of Trent teaches, the priest and victim are also one and the same:

> It is Christ Himself, the eternal high priest of the New Covenant who, acting through the ministry of the priests, offers the Eucharistic sacrifice. And it is the same Christ, really present under the species of bread and wine, who is the offering of the Eucharistic sacrifice.
>
> *CCC*, #1410

So, in reality there is only one Mass, one eternal Liturgy of the Eucharist, and it's taking place in heaven all the time. Christ, the One Great High Priest, is celebrating it, perpetually offering His once-for-all sacrifice to the Father in the heavenly court, surrounded by Mary and the saints, and by the angels, who sing His praise in endless adoration.

Wow!

We sit there in our parish church, locked in the confines of our own time and place, thinking that we're joining our priest in offering our own particular Mass. But, in reality, Christ is inviting us to enter in, beyond the veil, so that He can lift us up, out of time and into the Eternal Now, into the very sanctuary of heaven, where He leads us into the presence of the Father (See Hebrews 10:19-21).

As the *Catechism* explains it, our earthly liturgy "participates in the liturgy of heaven." Each Mass gives us

> a foretaste of that heavenly liturgy, ... where Christ is sitting at the right hand of God, Minister of the Sanctuary and of the true tabernacle. With all the warriors of the

heavenly army we sing a hymn of glory to
the Lord.

#1090

What an awesome reality! By *our* celebration of
the Mass in our little parish church, anytime, and
anywhere, "we already unite ourselves with the heavenly liturgy and anticipate eternal life" (#1326). Our
participation in the Holy Sacrifice allows us to slip
the bonds of time and place and "unites us even now
to the Church in heaven, the Blessed Virgin Mary,
and the saints" (#1419). We're not merely attending
Mass. We're joining with all of heaven and earth in
celebrating that one eternal liturgy!

I remember when these thoughts were first going
through my head. I used to share them with Fr.
George Kosicki after morning Mass. One particular
morning, when Father reached the end of the Preface
and said, "Now, let us join the choirs of angels as they
sing their unending hymn of praise," something just
clicked!

We looked at each other and knew that we were
both thinking the same thing: "Wow! That's what
we're really doing! It's not *my* 'Holy, Holy, Holy.' I'm

not singing my own little song of praise. I'm joining the song that the angels are singing all the time!"

St. Faustina often experienced this reality, not only during the liturgy, but also during times of adoration. In her prayer, "At the Feet of Christ in the Eucharist," she writes:

> Oh King of Glory, though You hide Your beauty, yet the eye of my soul rends the veil. I see the angelic choirs giving You honor without cease and all the heavenly powers praising You without cease, and without cease they are saying, "Holy, Holy, Holy!"

Diary, 80

Understanding all this, how can we ever consider a Mass "our" Mass? We are not praying alone, and we are not praying only with the other people in church with us. The Mass is the most complete experience of unity possible for us on earth, for we are praying together with the whole Church — all over the world *and in heaven.* So, no matter how much a particular celebration of the Mass falls short of what we would like it to be or feel it ought to be, *we should never lose sight of that wondrous liturgy in which the Mass allows us to participate.*

Theologian Scott Hahn, in his book *The Lamb's Supper* (which should be required reading for every Catholic), shows just how wondrous this heavenly liturgy is — and how real our participation in it is:

> We go to heaven when we go to Mass. This is not merely a symbol, not a metaphor, not a parable, not a figure of speech. It is real. ... We *do* go to heaven when we go to Mass, and this is true of *every* Mass we attend, regardless of the quality of the music or the fervor of the preaching. ... The Mass — and I mean *every* single Mass — is heaven on earth.

And what of the priest? Where is the priest in all this? If, as Hahn explains, "we are there with Jesus in heaven whenever we go to Mass," what is the role of the priest in this remarkable union of heaven and earth? Where does the priest fit in?

Pope John Paul II explains that the priesthood is inseparably linked to the Eucharist. To the priest has been given the most unique of all privileges, together with a profound responsibility, for "there can be no Eucharist without the priesthood, just as there can be no priesthood without the Eucharist."

Addressing his brother priests and bishops in *The Mystery and Worship of the Eucharist,* Pope John Paul II writes:

> Through our ordination — the cele-
> bration of which is linked to the Holy Mass
> from the very first liturgical evidence — we
> are united in a singular and exceptional way
> to the Eucharist. In a certain way we derive
> from it and exist for it. We are also, and in a
> special way, responsible for it.

The Holy Eucharist, continues Pope John Paul II, is "the greatest gift in the order of grace and of sacrament" that God has given us, and the Church has a special responsibility to protect and preserve its sacredness, especially as the sacrament of unity. Every priest who celebrates the Mass should remember that it is "not only he with his community," but the whole Church that is praying. Thus,

> the priest ... cannot consider himself a

"proprietor" who can make free use of the liturgical text and of the sacred rite as if it were his own property, in such a way as to stamp it with his own arbitrary personal style.

In *Gift and Mystery*, the pope's reflection on his own 50 years as a priest, he returns to this theme. The priest, he explains, is the "steward of the mysteries of God ... not the owner":

> The priest receives from Christ the treasures of salvation ... to distribute them among the people to whom he is sent. ... No one may consider himself the "owner" of these treasures; they are meant for all. But ... the priest has the task of administering them.

The Catechism of the Catholic Church confirms this teaching in a very clear way, explaining that, because of the sacredness of the liturgy,

> No sacramental rite may be modified or manipulated at the will of the minister or the community. Even the supreme authority in

the Church may not change the liturgy arbitrarily, but only in the obedience of faith and with religious respect for the mystery of the liturgy.

#1125

So if the priest's task is simply to "distribute the treasures," preserve the sacredness of the mystery of the Eucharist, and refrain from any kind of ownership or individualism that might detract from this sacrament of unity, where does his great privilege come in? Is he anything more than a spiritual robot for Christ and the Church?

As Pope John Paul II explains, the priest is called to be so completely and personally united to Christ as to become, in a very real sense, "another Christ:"

The priestly vocation is ... the mystery of a "wondrous exchange" ... between God and man. A man offers his humanity to Christ, so that Christ may use him as an instrument of salvation, making him as it were into another Christ.

Through his ordination, the priest is not merely authorized to represent Christ, but rather is uniquely and sacramentally identified with Him:

> The priest offers the Holy Sacrifice *in persona Christi;* this means more than offering "in the name of" or "in place of" Christ. *In persona* means in specific sacramental identification with "the eternal High Priest," who is the author and principal subject of this sacrifice of His, a sacrifice in which, in truth, nobody can take His place.

In celebrating the Eucharist, the priest is not saying his own individual Mass but, through this complete and personal identification with Christ, is able to re-present the one eternal Mass:

> Is there any greater fulfillment of our humanity than to be able to re-present every day *in persona Christi* the redemptive sacrifice, the same sacrifice that Christ offered on the cross? In this sacrifice, ... the very mystery of the Trinity is present in the most profound way, and ... the entire created universe is "united" (cf Eph 1:10 *RSV*).

$\mathscr{S}$ECRET 4

*The Eucharist is not just
one miracle.*

*What miracles! Who would ever
have imagined such! …
If the angels could be jealous of men,
they would be so for one reason:
Holy Communion.*

St. Maximilian Kolbe

W hen I was a child, with a very simple understanding and a very simple faith, miracles
were like magic to me. I had no idea how Christ did

SECRETS OF THE EUCHARIST

them, and I didn't really care. They were just "cool."

> Poof! Water turns to wine. Poof! A leper
> is healed. Poof! The wind stops. Poof! A
> dead man comes back to life.

I never thought about any of the things that might have had to happen in order for miracles like these to take place, never got into any of the complexities of a particular transformation. To my child's mind, each miracle was just a single, instantaneous action, like the wave of a wand — a wonderful piece of magic from the Great Magician.

And the Eucharist was the best of them all! I'd kneel in rapt attention, with my eyes fixed on the priest as he raised the Host.

"This is my body." Poof! What still looks like bread isn't bread anymore; it's Christ.

"This is my blood." Poof! It's not wine anymore; it's Christ.

And with quiet awe, I'd whisper St. Thomas' cry of faith: "My Lord and my God!" (Jn 20:28).

Thanks be to God, that child-like faith has never left me. I'm still in awe, and I still whisper those powerful words, every time.

But it's not just a great miracle to me any more. It's a whole bunch of them, all rolled into one. (How's that for a sophisticated theological definition?)

What began the change in my thinking was the teaching of Pope Leo XIII who, in his encyclical letter on the Eucharist, wrote:

> Indeed, in it alone are contained, in a remarkable richness and variety of miracles, all supernatural realities.

What powerful phrases! The Eucharist is so much more than we will ever be able to comprehend. Somehow it contains "all supernatural realities," and not just through one miracle, but through a "variety of miracles."

At the words of consecration, as Fr. Frederick Faber explains in his beautiful book, *The Blessed Sacrament,* there occurs

> ... a course of resplendent miracles, each more marvelous than a world's creation out of nothing.

These resplendent miracles do not happen in sequence, one after the other, but rather occur simultaneously for, as Fr. Faber explains:

> Here there has been no succession: in one and the same moment the whole range of these miracles was traversed and fulfilled.

What are all these miracles that happen together and are each more marvelous than the creation of the world?

I don't think we'll ever know the full answer to that question, at least not this side of heaven. As St. Faustina writes, "The miracles of mercy are impenetrable. Neither the sinner nor the just one will fathom them" (*Diary*, 1215).

But being able to list and fully understand this "variety of miracles" isn't the point. Simply by recognizing the complexities of the Eucharistic mystery and reflecting on whatever glimpses we catch of the miraculous, we can grow in our awareness of what a special gift we have been given.

And we have indeed caught glimpses of the miraculous. Think back on secrets 1-3:

✝ At the words of a mere creature, the bread and wine cease to exist, but all their scientific properties remain;

✝ Even the tiniest particle of what our senses still perceive as bread and wine is now Christ;

✝ Christ's presence is not symbolic or partial, but real and complete: He is present body, blood, soul, and divinity;

✝ Christ is truly present just as He is in heaven, alive and glorious;

✝ Christ does not leave heaven. His existence in heaven is not multiplied, but made present — not only in one place — but in every place where Mass is being celebrated;

✝ Only Christ is present sacramentally under the appearances of bread and wine, but He is not alone. The Father and the Holy Spirit and all of heaven are present with Him;

✝ During each celebration of the Mass, we are lifted out of time and into eternity to participate with the angels and saints in the one divine liturgy that is being continually celebrated in heaven as Christ offers His once-for-all sacrifice to the Father;

✝ The priest is united to the Eucharist in such a unique and exceptional way that he receives a "specific sacramental identification" with Christ, which thus enables him to offer the Holy Sacrifice in the person of Christ;

✝ Through the Eucharistic sacrifice, the "entire created universe is united."

All these miracles, together with perhaps many more that we don't even know about, take place instantly and simultaneously. And, if we return to Pope Leo XIII's statement, we find that, through these miracles, we receive — "in a remarkable richness" — "all supernatural realities."

St. Thomas Aquinas echoes this, explaining that the Eucharist contains "the Church's entire spiritual wealth" and thus is the "goal of all the sacraments."

The *Catechism* emphasizes the same truth:

The Eucharist is 'the source and summit of the Christian life' (*Lumen Gentium*). 'The other sacraments ... are bound up with the Eucharist and are oriented toward it. For in the blessed Eucharist is contained the whole spiritual good of the Church' (*Presbyterorum ordinis*).

#1324

No wonder Pope Paul VI referred to the Eucharist as not just a great mystery, but "*The* Mystery of Faith!" The Lord has given us more in this sacrament than we can possibly understand. "It is only in eternity," says St. Faustina, "that we shall know the great mystery effected in us by Holy Communion (*Diary*, 841)."

"The Eucharistic Sacrifice," explains Pope John Paul, is "a single sacrifice that embraces everything. It is the greatest treasure of the Church ... an inexpressible gift."

Thank you, Lord, for the miracles through which you give us this all-encompassing gift and for the miracles you accomplish in us when we receive it, as you "fill us with every heavenly blessing and grace" (*CCC* #1402).

$\mathscr{S}$ECRET 5

We don't just receive.

The Eucharist involves more than just receiving;
it also involves satisfying the hunger of Christ.
He says "Come to me." He is hungry for souls.
Nowhere does the Gospel say: "Go away,"
but always "come to me."

Mother Teresa

We saw earlier that the words we use can often get in our way, actually limiting our understanding of what they are intended to reflect. "Receive" is one of those words.

Just as the phrase "the Body of Christ" can suggest merely the human nature of Christ or the image of His dead body on the cross, so the phrase "receiving Communion" can suggest a passive reality. It can reinforce the concept that we're not really "doing" anything. God is the one who is doing; we are simply receiving.

But think back on what we've just seen about the incredible gift we're being offered, the awesome miracles that are taking place so that we can receive the fullness of God Himself. How can we receive such a gift in a merely passive way?

Yes, Christ is doing something. But part of what He's doing is calling to us, inviting us to respond to His initiative in an active way.

As Mother Teresa explains, Christ is "hungry for souls," and He is calling us to come to Him and satisfy that hunger. He is calling us not to merely receive Communion but to enter into communion.

How do we enter into communion?

One way to start is by taking a fresh look at the word communion itself.

It literally means "union with," or "completely

one." When used to denote the sacrament of the Eucharist, it suggests a similar union to that which is effected by the sacrament of marriage, where "the two become one flesh." As the *Catechism* explains, the Eucharist is called "Holy Communion"

> because by this sacrament we unite ourselves to Christ, who makes us sharers in his Body and Blood to form a single body.
>
> #1331

> All who eat the one broken bread, Christ, enter into communion with him and form but one body in him."
>
> #1329

Notice the actions in these quotes. "We *unite* ourselves to Christ" and "*enter* into communion with him." Just as a marriage takes active participation and "communication" from each person in order to achieve the desired union, so, too, the reception of the Eucharist. We can not leave it all up to God.

"Receiving Communion," writes Pope Benedict XVI, "means entering into communion with Jesus Christ. ... What is given us here is not a piece of a body, not a thing, but Him, the Resurrected one himself — the person who shares himself with us in his love. ...This means that receiving Communion is always a personal act. ... In Communion I enter into the Lord, who is communicating himself to me."

When I receive Communion properly, I am not merely receiving something into me; I am actively involved in the process, fully present to the One who is present within me, uniting my whole being with Him, becoming "one flesh" with Christ, and through Him entering into a uniquely personal encounter with the Father and the Holy Spirit as well:

> Through the celebration of the Eucharist, the faithful ... gain access to God the Father through the Son. They enter into communion with the most Holy Trinity.
>
> *Decree on Ecumenism*, 15

This "entering into" communion, this personal encounter with Christ and, through Him, with the other persons of the Trinity, doesn't simply involve God dwelling in us. It involves relationship. The indwelling of God is a gift demanding a reciprocal response. We must give ourselves to Christ as He gives Himself to us. Christ's plan is not merely to live in us, but also to enable us to live in Him: "Whoever eats my flesh and drinks my blood remains in me and I in him." (Jn 6:56)

St. Cyril of Jerusalem uses a very graphic image to convey this intimate union to which the Eucharist invites us:

> Throw melted wax into melted wax, and the one interpenetrates the other perfectly. In the same way, when the Body and Blood of Christ are received, the union is such that Christ is in the recipient and he in Christ.

"To respond to this invitation," the *Catechism* explains, "we must prepare ourselves for so great and so holy a moment" (#1385).

How do we prepare? The *Catechism* presents several minimum requirements:

✝ We must examine our consciences;

✝ If we are conscious of grave sin, we must go to confession before we receive Communion;

✝ We should reflect on our unworthiness and ask confidently for God's healing ("Lord I am not worthy, but only say the word and I shall be healed");

✝ We should observe the fast required by the Church;

✝ We should ensure that our "bodily demeanor," including our gestures and our clothing, "convey the respect, solemnity, and joy of this moment when Christ becomes our guest" (#1385-1387).

But beyond these minimum requirements, the Church has always emphasized the importance of a time of preparation before Communion and a time of thanksgiving after Communion to properly dispose our minds and hearts to be able to enter into the deeper relationship of mutual love and unity to which the sacrament calls us.

How seriously the saints took this! And what a

stark contrast there is between their preparations and thanksgivings and the all too prevalent tendency today to simply attend Mass, receive Communion, and leave immediately after the final blessing.

"The most solemn moment of my life," explained St. Faustina, "is the moment when I receive Holy Communion" (*Diary*, 1804). Conscious of the great importance of this moment, she always tried to make time for careful preparation, a time of recognizing who Christ is and running to meet Him, joining her heart to His.

> My soul is preparing for the coming of the Lord, who can do all things, who can make me perfect and holy. ... What am I and who are You, O Lord, King of eternal glory? O my heart, are you aware of who is coming to you today? ... I hear Him approaching. ... I go out to meet Him, and I invite Him to the dwelling place of my heart, humbling myself profoundly before His majesty. ... At the moment when I receive God, all my being is steeped in Him.
>
> *Diary*, 1825, 1810, 1806, 1814

St. Francis of Assisi, in a beautiful meditation on the Eucharist, exhorted his brothers to enter into communion with the same kind of humble and total giving of self:

> See the humility of God, brothers, and pour out your hearts before Him! Humble yourselves that you may be exalted by Him! Hold back nothing of yourselves for your-selves, that He who gives Himself totally to you may receive you totally!

After receiving Communion, many of the saints would spend an extended time of thanksgiving, during which they would receive great insights and often go into ecstasy.

"The minutes that follow Communion," wrote St. Mary Magdalene di Pazzi, "are the most precious we have in our lives." St. Teresa of Jesus urged her daughters not to rush out after Mass but to treasure the opportunity for thanksgiving: "Let us detain our-selves lovingly with Jesus," she said, "and not waste the hour that follows Communion." And St. Louis de Montfort wrote, "I would not give up this hour of

Thanksgiving even for an hour of Paradise."

Perhaps the best contemporary example of this complete entering into communion and the depths of union with God that can result from it is St. Padre Pio, canonized June 16, 2002. He wrote:

> When Mass was over I remained with Jesus in thanksgiving. Oh how sweet was the colloquy with paradise that morning! It was such that, although I want to tell you all about it, I cannot. ... The heart of Jesus and my own — allow me to use the expression — were fused. No longer were two hearts beating but only one. My own heart had disappeared, as a drop of water is lost in the ocean. Jesus was its paradise, its king. My joy was so intense and deep that I could bear it no more and tears of happiness poured down my cheeks.

*S*ECRET 6

Every reception is different.

The more resemblance there is between the person who goes to Communion and Jesus, so much the better will the fruits of Holy Communion be.

St. Anthony Mary Claret

This secret is really a continuation of Secret 5, because there is an absolute relationship between how I receive and what I receive. The more I am able to enter into communion, uniting myself with Jesus, the more fruitful my reception will be.

For most of my life, I viewed the reception of Communion as a specific action that was simply repeated at every Mass. It never occurred to me that there was anything different about receiving today from what there was yesterday or will be tomorrow. It goes back to that same passive mentality, the misconception that I'm not really doing anything. It's God who's doing something, and He does the same thing every time we receive. Right?

Wrong. In the last five chapters we have seen the "good news" about the wonderful things Christ wants to do for us through our reception of Communion, how He wants to flood us with miracles of grace and live in us as we live in Him.

Now here's the "bad news": None of it happens if our attitude isn't right. "In a false person," writes St. Thomas Aquinas, "the sacrament does not produce any effect."

That's a pretty strong statement. When's the last time you heard that preached from the pulpit?

Imagine if, just as people are starting to get up to go to Communion, the priest were to hold up his hand like a traffic cop and stop everyone:

Hold on a minute, folks! I know you all want to come up and receive, but I just want to remind you to examine yourselves first, because the sacrament won't have any effect if you're a false person.

Ouch! That could sure generate some interesting discussion in the parking lot after Mass — especially concerning the obvious question:

What's a "false" person?

St. Thomas explains:

We are false when the inmost self does not correspond to what is expressed externally. The sacrament of the Eucharist is an external sign that Christ is incorporated into the one who receives him and he into Christ. One is false if in his heart he does not desire this union and does not even try to remove every obstacle to it. Christ therefore does not remain in him, neither does he in Christ.

Wow! If when I receive, I'm not desiring this special sacramental union with Christ and trying to get rid of anything in my mind or heart that is blocking it, I gain none of the sacramental effect that Christ wants to give me. I'm still receiving the sacrament, but I get none of its fruit.

In his *Summa,* St. Thomas elaborates on this teaching, presenting a strong distinction between the sacrament itself and its effects. "A person receives the effect of this sacrament according to his condition," he explains, stressing that there is "no effect save on those who are united to the sacrament through faith and charity."

Comparing the Eucharist to the Passion of Christ, St. Thomas continues:

> As Christ's Passion does not produce its effect on those who do not hold him as they should, so also those do not attain heaven through this sacrament who receive him unworthily. Accordingly, Augustine writes, "The sacrament is one thing, its virtue another. Many receive from the altar and, receiving it, are dead. Eat therefore heavenly bread, carry innocence to the altar." So it is not surprising that those who do not keep a pure heart fail to gain the effect of the sacrament.

St. Paul goes a step further in his warning, emphasizing that, if our attitude is not right when we receive, we not only fail to gain the good fruit of the sacrament but can also harm ourselves spiritually:

> Whoever eats the bread or drinks the cup of the Lord unworthily will have to answer for the body and blood of the Lord. A person should examine himself, and so eat the bread and drink the cup. For anyone who eats and drinks without discerning the body, eats and drinks judgment on himself.
>
> 1 Cor 11:27-29

St. John Chrysostom is even more blunt and specific about the dangers of receiving unworthily:

> I beseech, beg, and implore that no one draw near to this sacred table with a sullied and corrupt conscience. Such an act, in fact, can never be called "communion," not even were we to touch the Lord's body a thousand times over, but "condemnation," "torment," and "increase of punishment."

These warnings find a frightening echo in the teachings of the Council of Trent, which declares:

> For no crime is there heavier punish-
> ment to be feared from God than for the
> unholy or irreligious use by the faithful of
> that which ... contains the very Author and
> Source of holiness.
>
> *De Euch.*, v.i.

So much for my years of thinking every reception is the same! In reality, each time I receive can be significantly different. My spiritual disposition before, during, and after receiving the sacrament will determine whether the sacrament will produce good fruit in me (in varying degrees), have no effect at all, or result in my condemnation.

Historically, this awareness has sometimes result-ed in people becoming unduly worried about their worthiness to receive. Due to fear, self-doubt, or an over-scrupulous nature, some have tended to abstain from receiving even when there was no valid reason to do so.

Obviously, this is not what God wants. Christ wants us to receive Him; that's why He instituted this sacrament so dramatically at the Last Supper in the Upper Room. And, to ensure that we would always be able to receive Him worthily, He instituted the Sacrament of Reconciliation in that same room on Easter Sunday (Jn 20: 19-23).

This is why the Church teaches that, if we are conscious of having committed serious sin, we must go to meet Christ in the confessional before receiving Him in the Eucharist (see *CCC* #1385). There our misery meets His mercy, and we are restored to grace, so that we can now more worthily enter into Communion with Him through the Eucharist.

When St. Paul issued his warning about receiving worthily, he wasn't implying that we shouldn't receive. He was simply exhorting us to examine ourselves in order to make sure we are "discerning the body" when we receive.

What does "discerning the body" mean? According to St. Thomas, it means "distinguishing it from other food," recognizing that Christ is truly present. We must strive never to consume this "Bread" absent-mindedly or casually as we might eat other food, but rather to prepare ourselves adequately for this awesome banquet where, with great reverence and gratitude, we take God Himself into us.

St. Augustine echoes this exhortation, emphasizing that our reception of Communion must be an act of worship of the God we are receiving. But he, too, is not suggesting that we should be afraid to receive. On the contrary, he adds a strong encouragement for us not only to receive but to receive every day:

> Let no one eat Christ's flesh before he first worships it. …

> This is our daily bread: take it daily that it may profit you daily.

So, we shouldn't be afraid to receive; we should simply resolve to receive well.

During the Mass, one of the prescribed prayers for the priest to say before Communion reveals the awareness of the possible good or bad effects of receiving, while providing us a model of the attitude we should have when we receive. It contains a personal profession of faith in the Lordship of Jesus Christ, in his love and mercy, and in his real presence in the Eucharist; along with a plea that, since the sacrament is about to be received in this spirit of faith, it may bring health, not judgment:

> Lord Jesus Christ, with faith in your love and mercy I eat your body and drink your blood. Let it not bring me condemnation, but health in mind and body.

For me, the awareness that "what I receive depends on how I receive" is not a negative thing. It's exciting! It means that every time I receive the Eucharist I can enter into communion with God in a more complete, personal, and fruitful way. It means that the better I can prepare for each reception, the more I really can receive "health in mind and body."

What I need to do every time, above all else, is recognize who God is, acknowledge my unworthiness to receive such a gift, and prepare my heart to enter into communion with Him, trusting in His merciful love for me. And so, over and over, I repeat the Church's age-old echo of the centurion's cry:

> O Lord, I am not worthy to receive you, but only say the word and I shall be healed.
>
> See Mt 8:8

$\mathcal{S}$ECRET 7

*There's no limit
to the number of times
we can receive.*

**The manner of receiving this sacrament
is twofold, spiritual and sacramental.**

St. Thomas Aquinas

No limit to how many times we can receive?
I love this secret because at first glance it seems
wrong, but, once understood, it emphasizes a wonderful truth. When I announce this secret during a
talk, I usually pause and look around to see how

people are reacting. I get some strange looks. Some people even shake theirs heads as if to say, "That's not true! Except for special circumstances, you can only receive twice a day."

You may be having the same thoughts as you read this. But hang in there with me and it'll come clear. Once again, it all hinges on the word "receive."

Let's back up a bit. What the last two chapters really come down to is that every time you and I go to receive Communion we have a choice between two ways of receiving.

Recognizing that Christ is calling us to a unique personal encounter with Him (along with the Father and the Holy Spirit), we can prepare ourselves with great care, trying to rid ourselves of any barriers or obstacles to this union, and seeking to enter into communion with Him. Or, as in the example we saw of the "false person," we can receive Christ without really desiring this union in our hearts and without even trying to remove the obstacles to it.

In his *Summa*. St. Thomas calls this two kinds of eating: sacramental and spiritual.

Sacramental eating is when I receive with at least

some understanding of the sacrament and some intent to receive it.

Spiritual eating is when my sacramental eating is accompanied by a real longing for union with Christ. I thus receive not only the sacrament itself but also the sacramental effect whereby I am spiritually joined to Christ in faith and love.

This is the choice that confronts you and me every time we go to Communion. We can receive merely sacramentally, approaching the altar in an absent-minded, mechanical way as creatures of habit, lining up like robots to fulfill some pre-set programming.

Or we can feed on His sacred Body and Blood both physically and spiritually, approaching with focused reverence and awe, grateful for this amazing gift and longing to unite ourselves with God.

Obviously, these are two extremes, with an infinite number of variations in between. According to St. Thomas, mere sacramental eating can be contrasted with perfect spiritual eating in the same way that an embryo is contrasted with an adult.

From the moment of conception, we each go through a continuing process of growth, passing through various stages in our journey toward full physical, mental, emotional, and spiritual maturity.

So, too, with our reception of the Eucharist. The goal, as we saw in the last chapter, is to grow in the way we receive, maturing in our awareness, understanding, and desire for union with Christ, so that every sacramental reception will result in a more complete spiritual Communion.

With me so far? Let's go a little deeper.

St. Thomas goes on to explain that this complete spiritual Communion can even take place when we are unable to receive sacramentally, because "the effect of a sacrament can be secured if it is received by desire."

Some people, he continues, "take this sacrament spiritually before they eat sacramentally," and by their "desire of receiving the actual sacrament," they thus "communicate spiritually, though not sacramentally."

What does this mean?

It means that, in addition to the times when we can actually receive the sacrament of the Eucharist, we can also receive spiritually through our desire for the sacrament, uniting our hearts to the Heart of

Jesus in the Eucharist.

This is the reality that is expressed in Secret 7. Yes, there is a limit to the number of times you and I can receive the Eucharist sacramentally, but there is no limit to the number of times we can receive spiritually.

Years ago, if I had read this, it wouldn't have impressed me much. Like most Catholics, I had heard about spiritual Communion, but I viewed it as some kind of "consolation prize." If, for one reason or another, you couldn't receive Communion, you could at least unite yourself to Christ through prayer.

There was certainly some value to this but, for me, the words "at least" implied that this was not real Communion.

As I learned more about the Eucharist and about what real Communion is, I came to understand that *spiritual Communion is not a substitute for sacramental Communion, but a very real anticipation and extension of its fruits.*

The saints provide us with wonderful models for this. St. Francis de Sales resolved to make a spiritual Communion at least every 15 minutes so that he could link all the events of the day to his reception of the Eucharist at Mass.

St. Maximilian Kolbe, in addition to his reception of the Eucharist, made frequent visits to the Blessed Sacrament, often more than ten times a day. But even this was not enough for him, so, like St. Francis de Sales, he resolved to enter into spiritual Communion "at least once every quarter hour."

Kolbe stressed what we've already seen from St. Thomas Aquinas, that the graces of the Eucharist are received in proportion to our spiritual condition, our desire to be united with God. And, since God always honors our desire for union with Him, these graces are not limited to sacramental Communion. "At times," Kolbe explained, "spiritual Communion brings the same graces as sacramental."

If this is true, then why do we ever need to receive sacramentally?

Because Kolbe isn't talking about "instead of," but "in addition to." As we saw above, *true spiritual Communion is always an anticipation or an extension of sacramental Communion.* Ideally, it is both.

Christ made it very clear that He wants us to

receive Him sacramentally. He did not say, "Unless you unite your heart with mine you will not have life in you." He said, "Unless you eat the flesh of the Son of Man and drink His blood, you do not have life within you" (Jn 6:53).

He did not say, "If you desire to commune with me, you will have eternal life." He said "Whoever eats my flesh and drinks my blood has eternal life" Jn 6:54).

He did not say, "Whoever imagines me coming into his heart remains in me and I in him." He said, "Whoever eats my flesh and drinks my blood remains in me and I in him" (Jn 6: 56).

Thus, there can be no substitute for regular sacramental Communion, and *our spiritual Communion must always have sacramental Communion as its goal.* As St. Thomas explains, spiritual Communion is not merely a desire to be close to God. It is when "a person believes in Christ *with a desire of receiving this sacrament.* This is not merely to feed on Christ spiritually, but also spiritually to feed on this sacrament."

Any desire for union with God will bring grace, but in order to receive the special sacramental graces of the Eucharist, this desire must include a specific intent to receive the sacrament itself and thus unite with the Eucharistic presence of Christ.

When received with this specific intent and with complete purity of heart, spiritual Communion can indeed bring "the same graces as sacramental." But these graces all flow from the sacrament and would be received in a much more complete way if the sacrament itself were received with the same purity of heart.

St. Thomas teaches this very specifically:

> The actual receiving of this sacrament produces the effect more fully than the desiring of it.
>
> Even by desiring it, a person receives grace whereby he is spiritually alive. ... [But] when the sacrament itself is really received, grace is increased and the life of the spirit perfected and made whole by union with God.

"Union with God." That's what it's all about. Sacramental Communion brings us into union with

God, and spiritual Communion helps keep us there. Understood in this way, spiritual Communion has immense value.

St. Catherine of Siena records a vision in which Christ Himself taught her the great value of spiritual Communion. She had begun to question whether her spiritual Communions had any real value compared to sacramental Communion. Suddenly, she saw Christ holding two chalices.

> In this golden chalice I put your sacramental communions. In this silver chalice I put your spiritual communions. Both chalices are quite pleasing to me.

Two great modern saints of the Eucharist, St. Padre Pio and St. Faustina, each appear to have reached a state of continuous, uninterrupted spiritual Communion, flowing from their daily sacramental reception of the Eucharist as an extension of its fruits.

Through her devotion to the merciful Heart of Jesus in the Eucharist, St. Faustina was able to enter into an unbroken relationship with God — a personal, moment-to-moment, heart-to-heart conversation with Jesus in the unity of the Trinity:

> Jesus, when you come to me in Holy Communion, You who together with the Father and the Holy Spirit have deigned to dwell in the little heaven of my heart, I try to keep you company throughout the day. I do not leave you alone for even a moment.
>
> *Diary,* 486

Her diary entry for September 29, 1937, barely a year before her death, is a powerful witness of the great value of spiritual Communion in extending the effects of sacramental Communion:

> I have come to know that Holy Communion remains in me until the next Holy Communion. A vivid and clearly felt presence of God continues in my soul. ... My heart is a living tabernacle in which the living Host is reserved. I have never sought God in some far-off place, but within myself. It is in the depths of my own being that I commune with my God.
>
> *Diary,* 1302

St. Padre Pio not only lived this way himself, but

prescribed it for others as well:

> In the course of the day, … call on Jesus, even in the midst of all your occupations.… He will come and will remain always united with your soul by means of His grace and His holy love.
>
> Fly with your spirit before the tabernacle, when you cannot stand before it bodily, and there pour out the ardent longings of your soul and embrace the Beloved of souls, even more than if you had been permitted to receive Him sacramentally.

"Even more than if you had been permitted to receive Him sacramentally." This phrase resounds within me, because it reminds me of several personal situations I have witnessed — situations that have inspired me but also shamed me for the times I have taken the Eucharist for granted.

I especially remember a young woman in the midst of a deep conversion experience, struggling with addiction, and longing for the grace to say a full yes to God. Times of spiritual victory alternated with moments of weakness and doubts that God could really love her. She was eager to begin a new way of life, but felt trapped by her past life, habits of sin, and the sense of her own inadequacy.

Overcoming her fear of going to confession, she had scheduled a meeting with a priest she felt she could talk to, but their schedules were such that the appointment was weeks away.

She was at Mass every morning, but refrained from going to Communion. When I'd return to the pew, I'd find her kneeling silently, with her eyes filled with tears.

One day, when I saw that she was still crying after Mass had ended, I gently put my hand on hers to comfort her. She turned and whispered through her tears, "I'm so sad that I can't receive Him."

I told her that she could receive Him. Her repentance, her decision to go to confession, her resolution to avoid sin, and the longing of her heart had already brought Him to her. Though she couldn't yet receive sacramentally, she was already receiving the graces of the sacrament through her desire to receive it, already beginning the new life of grace that would be hers in its fullness when she could receive sacramentally.

The tears still came at Communion time every day, but there was now joy mixed with the sadness. When she was finally able to receive the sacrament itself, she glowed with that joy, and I found myself in tears, inspired by her example and repenting of the times I had received so casually, without appreciating this great gift.

A similar situation involved a middle-aged man who had been away from the Church for many years. He had been married, but with no real awareness of marriage as a sacrament, and it had ended in divorce and remarriage outside of the Church. Years later, during a casual visit to a Marian apparition site, he experienced a powerful conversion that led him back to his Catholic faith with a real desire to learn it, live it, and receive the sacraments again. (Mary always leads us to the Eucharist.)

When I met him, he was attending daily Mass. He was longing to receive Communion, but was obediently refraining because the annulment he had filed for had not yet been granted.

It took four years. Every morning for four years he tried to make a good spiritual Communion as he watched others in the church receive sacramentally. Each time I was at Mass with him, I was humbled by his faith and obedience and inspired by his devotion to the Eucharist.

I found myself repenting again for the times I had taken the Eucharist for granted, and I was well aware that he was probably gaining more grace from the sacrament than many of us who were actually able to receive sacramentally.

The day he received word that his annulment had come through, he was like a little kid anticipating an ice cream cone. "Now," he said, beaming with joy, "I will finally be able to receive Him again!"

I almost envied him, but then realized that we can all have this same joy every day, not only at the times when we actually receive Communion, but at any time we choose to unite ourselves with Christ's Eucharistic presence.

How do we begin?

First of all, we can each resolve to make a good spiritual Communion any time we are unable to receive sacramentally at Mass. Many people over the years have used the great prayer of St. Alphonsus:

My Jesus, I believe that you are really present in the Most Holy Sacrament. I love you above all things, and I desire to possess you within my soul. Since I cannot now receive you sacramentally, come at least spiritually into my heart. I embrace you as being already there and unite myself wholly to you. Never permit me to be separated from you.

Or the traditional prayers approved by the Sacred Congregation of Indulgences:

O Jesus, I turn toward the holy tabernacle where you live hidden for love of me. I love you, O my God. I cannot receive you in Holy Communion. Come nevertheless and visit me with your grace. Come spiritually into my heart. Purify it. Sanctify it. Render it like unto your own.

Lord, I am not worthy that you should enter under my roof, but only say the word and my soul shall be healed.

Any other appropriate prayers may also be used,

or you can make up your own prayer. We can unite ourselves with Christ in the Eucharist at any time and in any way — through words, mental images, or simply what St. Therese called "a surge of the heart." I personally find that what helps me the most is to imagine myself withdrawing into my own heart, even for an instant, and meeting God there.

Sometimes there are no words. I just imagine the rays of mercy pouring into my heart from the Heart of Jesus in the Eucharist or on the cross. Sometimes I try to envision the rays reversing themselves, drawing me up through the Eucharistic Heart of Jesus into heaven. Or I imagine Mary visiting me as she did Elizabeth, bringing her Son into my heart.

If any words come to mind, I try to express them simply and naturally:

> Lord, Jesus, come into my Heart. ... Heal me, Jesus. ... Jesus, Mercy. ... Jesus, make my heart like Yours. ... Jesus, I trust in You. ... Mary, unite my heart to yours and to the Heart of Jesus.

What often comes to me is an image of the scene

I mentioned in Secret 1, when the Angel of Peace brought the Eucharist to the three children of Fatima and showed them how to adore God. I try to see the chalice and the Host suspended in the air and, with the angel, I throw myself prostrate on the ground and pray:

> O my God, I believe, I adore, I hope, and I love you. I ask pardon for all those who do not believe, do not adore, do not hope, do not love you.

I encourage you to begin this practice in whatever ways it feels natural for you. At times it may be 15-20 minutes in front of the Eucharist. At other times, it may be a brief instant in the midst of your daily work.

Frequency is much more important than duration, because the more you practice spiritual Communion, the more it becomes a habit, a natural instinct to unite yourself with God.

And there's no better way to grow spiritually. As St. Leonard of Port Maurice explains:

If you practice the holy exercise of spiritual Communion several times each day, within a month you will see your heart completely changed.

You'll find that every moment can become an occasion for making a spiritual communion. Distractions, temptations, anxieties, delays, the beginning or end of a task — all can become reminders of the need to renew your relationship with God, withdrawing for a moment to meet with Him in the depths of your heart.

And, in times of spiritual dryness, we can follow the prescription of St. John Vianney, the Cure of Ars:

A spiritual Communion acts on the soul as blowing does on a cinder-covered fire which was about to go out. Whenever you feel your love of God growing cold, quickly make a spiritual Communion.

"Quickly!" There's a sense of urgency here. The saints are trying to tell us that we should not limit our union with Christ in the Eucharist to sacramental

Communion once a week, or even once a day. We need Christ's living presence in our lives moment-by-moment to nourish us and protect us from sin, so we need to renew our union with Him regularly, especially any time we feel ourselves drifting away.

Christ is not merely present in this sacrament during Mass! The Eucharist is the ongoing fulfillment of Christ's Gospel promise to remain with us:

> Behold, I am with you always,
> until the end of the age.
>
> Mt 28:20

We are each called to enter into an unbroken relationship with God, and Christ remains with us in the Eucharist to make this possible. The purpose of the Eucharist is to transform us, to divinize us so that we become like Christ and are continually united with Him.

With each sacramental reception of Communion, we can become more and more transformed by grace into a real sharing in the way Christ lives. And by also entering frequently into spiritual Communion, we continue this process until the next time we are able to receive sacramentally.

This union with His children is God's great desire, but He won't force it on us. He waits for us to ask. Spiritual Communion is when we invite God to do what He wants to do: to come into our hearts with all of heaven and lift us beyond the veil into the eternity of His love.

What a wonderful thing it would be if we could all develop such a constant, daily practice of spiritual Communion that we could pray with St. Faustina:

> Oh Jesus, concealed in the Host, my sweet Master and faithful Friend, how happy my soul is to have such a Friend who always keeps me company. … How happy I am to be a dwelling place for you, O Lord! My heart is a temple in which you dwell continually.
>
> *Diary,* 877, 1392

NO LIMIT

AFTERWORD
Fr. Hal's Grits

**Take as many treasures
from My Heart
as you can carry.**

St. Faustina, Diary, 294

When you finished reading the last chapter, I hope it didn't seem like an ending, because we're still only at the beginning.

In the Foreword, I mentioned my sense of being on a spiritual treasure hunt for the precious gems of truth about the Eucharist. I've only shared seven of them with you here. In my talks at conferences and parish missions I sometimes discuss several others, and perhaps that will become the subject of another book, but even that will still be just a beginning. Exploring the mysteries of the Eucharist is like discovering a bottomless treasure chest; as you unpack each gem, it reveals another that was hidden from view. No matter how many you discover, there are always more.

Fr. Harold Cohen, a wonderful Jesuit priest from New Orleans, used to tell a great little story about the word *more*. As a true southern boy, he always loved his grits. His parents told him that his first word wasn't *ma-ma* or *da-da;* it was *more*. And what he wanted more of was grits.

Later on in his priestly life, the word took on a spiritual significance for him. Fr. Hal had learned that God always has more to give and always wants to give it. He just waits for us to ask.

Once greedy for grits, Fr. Hal now became greedy for grace, and the prayer most often on his lips was "More, Lord, more." One of his favorite saints was St. Faustina, and he loved to quote a passage from her

Diary that he called "Gathering the Gems."

Describing one of the many visions she had of Christ, she wrote:

> Precious pearls and diamonds were pouring forth from the wound in His Heart. I saw how a multitude of souls was gathering these gifts, but there was one soul who was closest to His Heart and she, knowing the greatness of these gifts, was gathering them with liberality, not only for herself, but others as well. The Savior said to me: **Behold the treasures of grace that flow down upon souls, but not all know how to take advantage of My generosity.**
>
> *Diary,* 1687

I pray that these 7 Secrets of the Eucharist will cause you to hunger for more and inspire you to continue the treasure hunt on your own with great excitement and expectation.

There are some wonderful resources available, and you'll find many of them in the Notes, Sources, and References section that follows.

But the best resource is Jesus Himself, present for

us, in Person, in the tabernacle. *Nothing will equal the value of spending time with Him,* simply being present to Him who is present for you.

In two of the last documents of his pontificate, Pope John Paul II issued a clear call for Eucharistic adoration, repeatedly stressing that our worship of the Eucharist must not be limited to the Mass:

> The worship of the Eucharist outside of the Mass is of inestimable value. ... It is the responsibility of pastors to encourage, also by their personal witness, the practice of Eucharistic adoration and exposition of the Blessed Sacrament in particular, as well as prayer of adoration before Christ present under the Eucharistic species. ...
>
> Of all devotions, that of adoring Jesus in the Blessed Sacrament is the greatest after the sacraments, the one dearest to God and the one most helpful to us.
>
> *Ecclesia de Eucharistia,* #25

> Let us take the time to kneel before Jesus present in the Eucharist. ... The presence of Jesus in the tabernacle must be a

kind of *magnetic pole* attracting an ever greater number of souls enamored of him, ready to wait patiently to hear his voice and … to sense the beating of his heart.

Mane Nobiscum Domine, #18

Following the example of St Faustina and so many other saints, we must not only learn about the Eucharist; we must each develop and nourish a personal relationship with our Eucharistic Lord:

I spend every free moment at the feet of the hidden God. He is my Master; I ask Him about everything; I speak to Him about everything. Here I obtain strength and light; here I learn everything; here I am given light on how to act toward my neighbor. … I have enclosed myself in the tabernacle together with Jesus.

Diary, 704

Notes, Sources and References

SECRET 1

The Eucharist is alive.

Page 10: "Most Holy Trinity …" Msgr. William McGrath, "The Lady of the Rosary," *A Woman Clothed with the Sun* (Garden City, NY: Doubleday, 1961), p. 180.

Page 12: "… need to cultivate a lively awareness …" Pope John Paul II, *Mane Nobiscum Domine* (Stay with us, Lord), #18.

Page 13: "… exercise tolerance and to recognize

the decision of each person ..." Joseph Cardinal Ratzinger (Pope Benedict XVI), *God is Near Us* (San Francisco: Ignatius Press), pp. 69-70. He goes on to point out that "until the ninth century Communion was received in the hand, standing," but then explains that this doesn't mean it always has to be that way, because the Church is always "growing, maturing, understanding the mystery more profoundly."

Thus the new ritual of kneeling and receiving on the tongue, which was introduced in the ninth century, was also "quite justified, as an expression of reverence, and is well founded." But certainly, "the Church could not possibly have been celebrating the Eucharist unworthily for nine hundred years" (p. 70).

The rituals authorized by the Church may well continue to change as the Church continues to mature. What must always remain is reverence for the real presence and tolerance for the various ways of expressing that reverence, for in the dispute that "has broken out concerning the Eucharist ... the opposition of one party to another threatens to obscure the central mystery of the Church" (p. 57).

As an example of the spirit of reverence taught by

the early Fathers of the Church, Cardinal Ratzinger explains the catechetical teaching of St. Cyril of Jerusalem in the fourth century concerning the way people should receive: "They should make a throne of their hands, laying the right upon the left to form a throne for the King, forming at the same time a cross. This symbolic gesture, so fine and so profound, is what concerns him: the hands of man form a cross, which becomes a throne, down into which the King inclines himself. The open, outstretched hand can thus become a sign of the way that a man offers himself to the Lord, opens his hands for him, that they may become an instrument of his presence and a throne of his mercies in this world" (p. 70).

Page 13: "It is quite wrong to argue about this or that form of behavior." Joseph Cardinal Ratzinger (Pope Benedict XVI), *God is Near Us*, p. 71. The pope goes on to urge that instead of arguing about the outer forms or rituals of receiving Communion, we "should be concerned only to argue in favor of "a reverence in the heart, an inner submission before the mystery of God who puts himself into our hands."

He admonishes us "not to forget that not only our hands are impure but also our tongue and also our heart and that we often sin more with the tongue than with our hands." He explains that, by coming to us in Communion, "God takes an enormous risk ... allowing not only our hand and our tongue but even our heart to come into contact with him. We see this in the Lord's willingness to enter into us and live with us, within us, and to become from within the heart of our life and the agent of its transformation" (p. 71).

Page 14: "The flesh of the Son of Man ..." Pope John Paul II, *Ecclesia de Eucharistia* (Encyclical Letter on the Eucharist in its Relationship to the Church), #18.

SECRET 2

Christ is not alone.

Page 28: "The Word comes to us." Father M.V. Bernadot, O.P., *The Eucharist and the Trinity* (Wilmington, DE: Michael Glazier, 1977), p. 21.

Page 32: "God the Trinity comes to meet us, …" Stephan Otto Horn and Vinzenz Pfnur, editors, Joseph Cardinal Ratzinger, *God is Near Us*, p. 8.

Page 34: "Would it not have been enough …" St. Catherine of Siena, cited by Father M.V. Bernadot, O.P., *The Eucharist and the Trinity,* p. 26.

Page 34: "the whole celestial court … he saw the heavens open, …" Alberto D'Apolito, *Padre Pio of Pietrelcina, Memories, Experiences,* cited by Joan Carter McHugh, *My Daily Eucharist* (Lake Forest, IL: Witness), May 28.

Page 35: "It was beyond …" St. Therese of Lisieux, *The Story of a Soul* (New York: Doubleday, 1989), p. 52.

SECRET 3
Only one Mass.

Page 41: "[The Paschal Mystery is] ... 'once for all.'" See Rom 6:10; Heb 7:27; 9:12; Jn 13:1; 17:1.

Page 47: "We go to heaven ..." Scott Hahn, *The Lamb's Supper: The Mass as Heaven on Earth* (New York: Doubleday), 1999, pp. 5, 128.

Page 47: "We are there ..." Scott Hahn, *The Lamb's Supper: The Mass as Heaven on Earth, p. 125.*

Page 48: "...there can be no Eucharist without the priesthood ..." Pope John Paul II, *Gift and Mystery* (New York: Doubleday, 1996), pp. 77-78. Earlier the pope had explained that "it is precisely in the presence of the Eucharist that we understand and appreciate best the gift of the priesthood, for the two are inseparable." Homily in Korea, October 7, 1989.

Page 48: "Through our ordination ..." Pope John Paul II, *Dominicae Cenae* (On the Mystery and

NOTES, SOURCES AND REFERENCES

Worship of the Eucharist), February 24, 1980, #1.

Page 48: ..."the greatest gift in the order of grace ..." Pope John Paul II, *Dominicae Cenae*, #12.

Page 48: "...not only he with his community, ..." Pope John Paul II, *Dominicae Cenae*, #12.

Page 48: "The priest ..." Pope John Paul II, *Dominicae Cenae*, #12.

Page 49: "The priest receives from Christ ..." Pope John Paul II, *Gift and Mystery* (New York: Doubleday, 1996), pp. 72.

Page 50: "The priestly vocation ..." Pope John Paul II, *Gift and Mystery*, pp. 72-73.

Page 51: "The priest offers ..." Pope John Paul II, *Dominicae Cenae*, #8.

Page 51: "Is there any greater fulfillment ..." Pope John Paul II, *Gift and Mystery*, pp. 73.

SECRET 4

Not just one miracle.

Page 53: "What Miracles!" St. Maximilian Kolbe, SK III, 1145, p. 326, cited by Jerzy Domanski, OFM Conv., *For the Life of the World*, translated by Peter D. Fehlner, FI (Libertyville, IL: Academy of the Immaculate, 1993), p. 127.

Page 55: "Indeed, in it alone are contained ..." Pope Leo XIII, Encyclical Letter *Mirae caritatis*, cited by Pope Paul VI, *Mysterium Fidei* (The Mystery of Faith), #15.

Page 55: "A course of resplendent miracles, ..." Fr. Frederick Faber, *The Blessed Sacrament* (Rockford, IL:Tan Books, 1978), p. 128.

Page 56: "Here there has been no succession ..." Fr. Frederick Faber, *The Blessed Sacrament*, p. 128. For a more detailed and technical discussion of the various types of miracles involved, see pages 57-73, in which Fr. Faber identifies twelve miracles, two concerning "the substance of the bread and wine, two more the species, six the Body of our Lord and its concomitants, and two the consecrator in the Mass" (p. 59).

Page 58: "The Church's entire spiritual wealth." St. Thomas Aquinas, *Summa Theologiae*, q. 73, a. 3c.

Page 59: "No wonder Pope Paul VI referred to the Eucharist ..." *Mysterium Fidei* (The Mystery of Faith), September 3, 1965.

Page 59: "The Eucharistic Sacrifice ..." Pope John Paul II, *Prayer on Holy Thursday*, 1982, #1.

SECRET 5
We don't just receive.

Page 61: "The Eucharist involves more than just receiving." *Mother Teresa, A Life for God: The Mother Teresa Reader*, compiled by LaVonne Neff (Ann Arbor, MI: Servant Publications, 1995), p. 180.

Page 62: "…hungry for souls." *Mother Teresa, A Life for God*, p. 180.

Page 63: "Receiving Communion means …" Joseph Cardinal Ratzinger (Pope Benedict XVI), *God is Near Us* (San Francisco: Ignatius Press, 2003), p. 81.

Page 65: "Throw melted wax into melted wax, …" St. Cyril of Jerusalem, cited by Father M.V. Bernadot, O.P., *The Eucharist and the Trinity*, p. 17.

Page 68: "See the humility of God …" St. Francis of Assisi, "Letter to a General Chapter," in Regis J. Armstrong, OFM Cap., *St. Francis of Assisi: Writings for a Gospel Life* (New York: Crossroad Publishing, 1994), pp. 218-219.

Page 68: "The minutes that follow Communion are the most precious ..." St. Mary Magdalene di Pazzi, cited by Fr. Stefano M. Manelli, FI, *Jesus Our Eucharistic Love* (New Bedford, MA: Franciscan Friars of the Immaculate, 1996), p. 37.

Page 68: "Let us detain ourselves lovingly with Jesus ..." St. Teresa of Jesus, cited by Fr. Stefano M. Manelli, FI, *Jesus Our Eucharistic Love,* p. 37.

Page 68: "I would not give up this hour of thanks-giving ..." St. Louis de Montfort, cited by Fr. Stefano M. Manelli, FI, *Jesus Our Eucharistic Love,* p. 37.

Page 69: "When Mass was over I remained with Jesus in thanksgiving." St. Padre Pio, Letter to Padre Agostino, April 18, 1912, as cited by Fr. Benedict J. Groeschel, CFR, *Praying in the Presence of Our Lord* (Huntington, Indiana: Our Sunday Visitor, 1999), p. 35.

SECRET 6

Every reception is different.

Page 71: "The more resemblance there is ..." St. Anthony Mary Claret, cited by Fr. Stefano M. Manelli, FI, *Jesus Our Eucharistic Love,* p. 33.

Page 72: "In a false person, the sacrament does not produce any effect." St. Thomas Aquinas, Commentary on the Gospel of John 6:57, as cited by Chiara Lubich, *The Eucharist* (New York: New City Press, 1977), p. 73.

Page 73: "We are false when the inmost self ..." St. Thomas Aquinas, Commentary on the Gospel of John 6:57, as cited by Chiara Lubich, *The Eucharist,* p. 73.

Page 74: "A person receives the effect ..." St. Thomas Aquinas, *Summa Theologiae III,* q. 79, art. 6, reply: 1.

Page 74: "... no effect save on those who are united

to the sacrament through faith and charity." St. Thomas Aquinas, *Summa Theologiae III*, q. 79, art. 7, reply: 2.

Page 74: "As Christ's Passion does not produce its effect ..." St. Thomas Aquinas, *Summa Theologiae III*, q. 79, art. 2, reply: 2.

Page 75: "I beseech, beg, and implore ..." St. John Chrysostom, *Homily in Isaiam*, 6,3: PG 56, 139.

Page 77: "... distinguishing it from other food." St. Thomas Aquinas, *Summa Theologiae III*, q. 80, art. 5, reply: 2

Page 78: "Let no one eat Christ's flesh before he first worships it." St. Augustine in "Ps. XCVIII. 5" cited by St. Thomas Aquinas, *Summa Theologiae III*, q. 80, art. 6, reply: 2.

Page 78: "This is our daily bread ..." St. Augustine, *Sermon suppos.* LXXXIV. PL 39, 1908.

SECRET 7
No limit

Page 81: "The manner of receiving this sacrament is twofold …" St. Thomas Aquinas, *Summa Theologiae III*, q. 80, art. 11, reply.

Page 82: "Except for special circumstances …" See Code of Canon Law, Can. 917, and interpretation of the Canon by the Pont. Council for Legislative Texts, on July 11, 1984, clarifying that the Eucharist can only be received twice.

Page 82: "St. Thomas calls this two kinds of eating … spiritually joined to Christ in faith and love." See *Summa Theologiae III*, q. 80, art. 1, reply.

Page 83: "…mere sacramental eating can be contrasted with perfect spiritual eating …" See *Summa Theologiae III*, q. 80, art. 1, reply.

Page 84: "… the effect of a sacrament can be

secured … " St. Thomas Aquinas, *Summa Theologiae III*, q. 80, art. 1, reply: 3. See also q. 79, art. 1, reply 1.

Page 85: "St. Francis de Sales … " See Fr. Stefano M. Manelli, FI, *Jesus Our Eucharistic Love*, p. 52.

Page 86: "… at least once every quarter hour." St. Maximilian Kolbe, SK III, 987 I, p. 720, cited by Jerzy Domanski, OFM Conv., *For the Life of the World*, p. 120.

Page 86: "At times, spiritual communion brings the same graces …" St. Maximilian Kolbe, SK II, 968, p. 647, cited by Jerzy Domanski, OFM Conv., *For the Life of the World*, p. 120.

Page 87: "… a person believes in Christ with a desire of receiving the sacrament." St. Thomas Aquinas, *Summa Theologiae III*, q. 80, art. 2, reply.

Page 88: "The actual receiving of this sacrament …" St. Thomas Aquinas, *Summa Theologiae III*, q. 80, art. 1, reply: 3.

Page 88: "Even by desiring it,…" St. Thomas Aquinas, *Summa Theologiae III,* q. 79, art. 1, reply: 1.

Page 89: "In this golden chalice … " St. Catherine of Siena, cited by Fr. Stefano M. Manelli, FI, *Jesus Our Eucharistic Love,* p. 50-51.

Page 91: "In the course of the day,… " St. Padre Pio, cited by Fr. Stefano M. Manelli, FI, *Jesus Our Eucharistic Love,* p. 51-52.

Page 95: "My Jesus, I believe … " St. Alphonsus Liguori, *The Holy Eucharist* (Brooklyn, NY: Redemptorist Fathers, 1934), p. 124.

Page 95: "O Jesus, I turn toward the holy tabernacle … " Sacred Congregation of Indulgences, *Rescript of November 24, 1922.*

Page 95: "Lord, I am not worthy …" Roman Missal, *The Raccolta* (New York: Benzinger Brothers, 1946), #129, p. 78.

Page 96: "A surge of the heart." St. Therese, *The Story of a Soul* (New York: Doubleday, 1957), p. 136.

Page 97: "O my God, I believe …" Msgr. William McGrath, "The Lady of the Rosary," *A Woman Clothed with the Sun*, p. 179.

Page 98: "If you practice the holy exercise of spiritual Communion …" St. Leonard of Port Maurice cited by Fr. Stefano M. Manelli, FI, *Jesus Our Eucharistic Love*, p. 53.

Page 98: "A spiritual Communion acts on the soul …" St. John Vianney, "On Frequent Communion," *Catechetical Instructions*, as cited by Fr. Wilfred Hurley, *Catholic Devotional Life* (St. Paul Editions, 1965). See also http://www.ewtn.com/library/CATECHSM/CATARS.htm.

More Books, CDs, & DVDs
from Vinny Fylnn and MercySong

7 Secrets of the Eucharist

This best-selling book by Vinny Flynn will give you a completely new awareness that the Eucharist is not just about receiving Communion; it's about transforming your daily life. Over 150,000 copies sold.

English Book **$9.95**   Audiobook (2 CDs) **$16.95**
Study Guide **$6.95**   Spanish Book **$9.95**

7 Secrets of Confession

In this second book of the "7 Secrets" series, Vinny Flynn presents what to many will be a whole new way of going to Confession, and invites you to begin an exciting personal journey to healing and holiness.

English Book **$12.95**   Audiobook (4 CDs) **$17.95**
Study Guide **$7.95**   Spanish Book **$12.95**

7 Secrets of Divine Mercy

Vinny Flynn draws from Scripture, the teachings of the Church, and the *Diary of St. Faustina* to show us how everything in our lives can become more meaningful, powerful, and life-changing once we really understand and embrace the gift of Divine Mercy.

English Book **$14.95**   Study Guide **$7.95**
Spanish Book **$14.95**

21 Ways to Worship:
A Guide to Eucharistic Adoration

Written in the author's personal, conversational style, *21 Ways to Worship* is an easy to read, practical guide, jam-packed with inspiring ideas, techniques, and prayers to help you grow in your personal relationship with God — during Adoration or any other time.

English Book **$14.95**   Spanish Book **$14.95**

Order online at www.mercysong.com

Mercy's Gaze:
100 Readings from Scripture & the *Diary of St. Faustina*

Compiled by Vinny Flynn, *Mercy's Gaze* breaks new ground as a first-ever themed collection of related Scripture and *Diary* passages. Rich spiritual fare for 100 days of prayer and reflection, with the *Diary* revealed as a Gospel of Mercy. **$14.95**

Parenting on Purpose:
7 Ways to Raise Terrific Christian Kids

Often funny, sometimes sad, and always engaging, this "how-to" book by Jason Free is a straightforward and practical sharing of specific ways to guide your children (or grandchildren) to a lasting and fulfilling relationship with God. **$14.95**

LIVE VIDEO PRESENTATIONS

Powerful, dynamic teachings by Vinny Flynn. Perfect for individual use, parish retreats, religious education classes, and spiritual formation groups!

7 Secrets of the Eucharist DVD

Live video of Vinny Flynn's powerful talk on the Eucharist, based on his widely-acclaimed book.

Includes 2 bonus secrets not found in the book. DVD: **$14.95**

7 Secrets of Confession DVD

Vinny Flynn's inspiring talk on confession, based on his best-selling book.

DVD: **$14.95**

Responding to God, Person to Person DVD

A Complete Parish Mission. Vinny's down-to-earth style and powerful teachings on the Sacraments, Divine Mercy, and the Father's love will inspire and revitalize your faith and draw you into a personal relationship with God that will change your life.

3 Talks on DVD: **$19.95**

DEVOTIONAL CDs

Benedictus
Traditional Holy Hour hymns with new arrangements and an Irish touch. Perfect for Holy Hours, healing services, Adoration, or quiet prayer time.

$15.99

The Rosary & The Chaplet of Divine Mercy
Our best-selling CD. Includes recited versions of the Rosary and the Chaplet, with powerful meditations on the Passion from St. Faustina's diary. $15.99

Chaplet of Divine Mercy
The traditional chant version sung by Vinny Flynn & daughters Colleen & Erin, featured for many years on EWTN. Over 80,000 copies sold.

English CD **$15.99**   Spanish CD **$14.99**

Mother of Mercy Scriptural Rosary
This award-winning album by Vinny Flynn & Still Waters features a brief scripture reading before each Hail Mary to help you stay focused on the mysteries. Includes all 20 mysteries with beautiful background instrumental music.

2 CDs **$17.99**   Pocket-sized Booklet **$6.95**

The Gospel Rosary of Pope John Paul II
Our most complete rosary set, featuring long & short versions of each of the 20 mysteries. Dramatic readings from scripture, accompanied by beautiful background music, draw you into the Gospel events.   4 CDs **$29.99**

The Complete Still Waters Rosary
A top seller. The short versions from each CD of the Gospel Rosary, remastered to fit on a single CD. Includes a brief meditation on each of the 20 mysteries. $15.99

BRING VINNY FLYNN TO YOUR PARISH

Powerful Catholic Teachings , Music, and Prayer

Whether it's for a single talk at a conference or church event, a series of presentations for a retreat, or a full-blown parish mission, Vinny Flynn will help draw you to a fuller understanding of the truths of our faith and a deeper personal relationship with God.

Vinny Flynn: Catholic teacher, musician, and author of *7 Secrets of the Eucharist*

- Eucharistic Night of Healing
- Divine Mercy retreats
- Reconciliation evenings
- Parish Missions

For complete details, including parish program outline, talk descriptions, booking form, and promotional materials, go to: www.vinnyflynn.com.